LORD HEAL ME

LORD HEAL ME

Personal Prayers

JOHN GUNSTONE

HIGHLAND BOOKS

Copyright © John Gunstone 1988
This edition 1988

Printed in Great Britain for
HIGHLAND BOOKS
Broadway House, The Broadway
Crowborough, East Sussex
by Richard Clay Ltd, Bungay, Suffolk
Typeset by CST, Eastbourne, E. Sussex.

CONTENTS

ACKNOWLEDGMENT

The Scripture quotations in this book are from The Holy Bible, *New International Version*, Copyright © 1973, 1978, 1984, by the International Bible Society. Published by Hodder and Stoughton and used with permission.

Other acknowledgments are printed on pages 127-128

INTRODUCTION

We believe that Jesus Christ is our Saviour, and in that faith we pray for the forgiveness of our sins. We also believe that he is our Healer. But we often find it difficult to pray with the same faith for healing – particularly for ourselves. I hope this book will help you to do that.

These prayers can be used as they are printed; but my intention is that they should be only models. Start with what I have written; then let the Holy Spirit lead you into using your own words, giving you discernment into how you should pray.

About half of the prayers in Parts 1 – 5 are taken from my *Prayers for Healing* (Highland Books, 1987), though many have been revised.

Part 6 contains suggestions for morning and evening prayers.

In Part 7 I have collected together twenty prayers written by others.

PART 1

AT HOME

Often it is at home where we first become aware of an illness developing. And it is at home that we recover, looked after by our family and friends. Home, then, is the best place for us to learn how to pray for healing.

And it is also the place where we can serve in Jesus Christ's name those who look after us. As they tidy our bed, bring us meals, and do the hundred-and-one jobs that we require, we can listen as they tell us about the things that concern them, and use our enforced time of rest to pray for them.

1 At Home

Lord Jesus,
 you shared the life of an earthly
  home at Nazareth
 and visited the homes of your friends.
Come into my home
 and touch me in this illness.
Restore me to health and wholeness
 to the praise of your holy name.

2   **A child's prayer**

Jesus, our Lord,
 you became a child to save us.
Hold me in your arms.
Give me your peace,
 and make me better,
  for your name's sake.

3   A young person's prayer

Thank you, Father God,
   for my parents and my family,
      for all that they have given me.
Help me, and help them,
   as our relationship changes.
Give me grace to love them
   as their maturing child,
      that we may grow together
         as your children.

Heal in me any hidden memories
   and unconscious fears
      which I may have received
         in my earlier years.
May your Holy Spirit inwardly cleanse me
   from things which spoil my walk
      with your Son
      and which ruin my friendships.
Protect me from evil influences,
   and enable me to be a light of your
      truth and love
      among my family, my friends,
         and my acquaintances.

I ask this in the name of Jesus Christ,
   my Saviour and Lord,
      that you, Father, may be glorified
         in me and in them.

4   For sick members of a family

Almighty and ever-loving Father,
   you bring health and salvation to all who
      believe in you.
I ask for your loving help
   for the sick in my family.

Send us your Spirit with gifts of strength
   and healing.
Enable us to put on your spiritual armour,
   that we may take our stand
      against the devil's schemes.

Restore them to wholeness,
   so that together we may follow
      Jesus your Son
      as we minister to those around us.

And may our home be a refuge
   where others find his healing and strength,
      because we have known your grace
         and grown in your love.

I offer this prayer to you in the name
   of Jesus Christ.

5 During a long illness

Father, teach me to wait patiently
　　for the fulfilment of your will in me.

I look to you for love and mercy,
　　compassion and grace.

Show me how to share in the sufferings of
　　　your beloved Son,
　　and to know his risen power.

Take away everything which prevents
　　　me from receiving
　　the healing gifts of your Spirit.

Help me to accept your agenda and your
　　　timetable for my life,
　　and to set aside my own.

I rejoice in your goodness to me,
　　in Jesus Christ.

6   Older members

All praise and glory are yours,
   Lord our God,
      for you have called us to serve you in love.

Thank you for the years you have given me
   in this family.
Thank you for what you have done for me
   in the past,
   and for what you are doing for me now
      as I look towards your future

Give me strength and courage as an
   elder brother/sister
   to continue to follow Jesus your Son,
      with the opportunities of old age.

And may I, through your grace,
   encourage the younger members
      of the family
      to be your faithful disciples.

I ask this through Christ our Lord.

7   **Medical Attention**

Jesus, great Physician,
  I have prayed for healing
    and you have sent to me this doctor.
Supporting him are many who serve you
  through medical, research, pharmacy,
    administrative and practical skills.

Enable me to accept his service to me
  as an agent of your healing power.
Guide him in his diagnosis
  and grant that without fear or hesitation
  I may cooperate with him
    in his decisions and prescriptions.

And I pray that, through the treatment
  I receive,
  you will heal me.
    and bless the doctor
and those involved with him in caring for me.

8   Carers

Heavenly Father, I praise you
    for those you send to look after me.
        especially the members of my family.

They need patience to cope with my demands,
    and compassion to accept me
        when I am full of self-pity and complaints.

Help me through this illness to die to
    myself each day,
    and, in your Spirit, to be raised with Christ,
        setting my heart on things above.

Grant me patience and thankfulness
    in receiving all that is done for me
        by those around me.
May our relationship grow in kindness
    and humility,
    and may we be bound together in your love.

I thank you, in the name of our Saviour,
    Jesus Christ,
    that through their care
        you are giving me your healing
        and renewing us in your Spirit,
            for your honour and glory.

9 Thanksgiving

Thanksgiving and praise be to you,
  heavenly Father
  for the love you give me in so many
    different ways.

I thank you for my family,
  my friends and neighbours,
  and the members of my church.

I thank you for teaching me
  how to be sorry for my faults,
    how to forgive, how to receive forgiveness
  and how to receive your healing
    by the power of your gracious Spirit.

I thank you for the varied abilities and gifts
  you have bestowed on us,
    to share with one another
    and to use for your purposes.

I thank you for difficult times
  as well as happy ones,
    and for all you showed me through them.

May our home be a little community
  where Jesus Christ is worshipped
    and where your kingdom is honoured.

10 Praise

Jesus, you invited your disciples
   to call you their friend.

I praise you that among my friends
   you have revealed your love
     in mending broken relationships,
     in bestowing gifts of healing,
   and in sharing your word.

May we be a company of those
   who follow your way to the cross,
     who are witnesses of your resurrection,
   and who receive the fulness of your Spirit.

Send us, as the Father sent you,
   for the glory of your name
     and the extension of your kingdom,
in the power of the Holy Spirit.

Praise be to you, Lord Jesus, for ever.

PART 2

IN HOSPITAL

It's difficult to pray when we're patients in a hospital ward. Besides the anxiety, and perhaps the discomfort, we are distracted by the incessant activities, the comings and goings, as well as the need to learn new routines. Drugs sometimes have peculiar side-effects on us. Relationships with others – an insensitive member of staff, or a difficult neighbour in the next bed – can occasionally darken our horizon.

Perhaps we can find ways of weaving our prayers into the timetable of the ward, in the quiet moments when the patients are dozing in their beds or watching the TV in the dayroom. Try praying during the night when you can't sleep, particularly for those around you and for the staff who are on duty.

Remember, as hospital patients we are in a place where God's healing gifts abound and where Christ's compassion for the sick is often manifested, even by those who do not acknowledge him as their Lord and Saviour.

Don't attempt to spend too long on your prayers. A few brief moments interspersed through the day will probably be as much as you can manage. If you don't feel like reading much, use only one or two of these prayers and then let the Holy Spirit direct your thoughts and meditations.

Don't worry if you are often distracted. The Lord understands. And don't feel guilty if you doze off in the middle of your prayers. Sleep is a great healing gift from God. In the Scriptures there are many occasions when God spoke to his servants as they slept.

1   Going into hospital

Jesus our Saviour,
make yourself known to me
   as I enter the hospital.

Help me to adjust to this new manner of life.

Give me gratitude for those who care for me,
   compassion for those in the ward with me,
   and love for them all.

2   Self-offering

Teach me, Lord God, to offer my body
  as a living sacrifice to you:
    my head, my arms, my legs;
    my conscious and my unconscious –
      impulses, thoughts, desires, ambitions –
    all the known and unknown
      that make up the real me.

Teach me, also, to offer those parts of my body
  which are sick and disabled.
Cleanse me, heal me, and renew me
  by your Spirit.

Through the offering of your beloved Son
  on the cross of Calvary,
    may the offering of my body
      be a spiritual act of worship.
      holy and pleasing to you.

3   During medical treatment

Almighty God, eternal and compassionate,
   giver of life and bringer of health,
grant that those who minister to me
   in medical and nursing care
    may be blessed in their work.

Enable me to cooperate with them
   as we reach out for your healing.

As my weakness is banished
   and my health is restored,
may I live by your Spirit
   to glorify your holy name
     through Jesus Christ.

4 In pain

Father, come to me.
I give you every part of my aching body.
I rest in your mercy and love.

In the name of Jesus, I ask you
 to lift this pain from me.

Deliver me from all evil.
Anoint me with your peace.
Glory to you, Lord, for ever.

5   Before an operation

Loving Father,
I put myself into your hands.
Deliver me from fear of pain and
   of the unknown.

Set the love of your dear Son over me,
   and guide with your wise Spirit
     the surgeon, the anaesthetist,
     and the theatre staff.
Anoint them as servants of your healing
   power.

And while I am unconscious
   may my deepest thoughts and feelings
     rest in you.
May I sleep in your peace
   and awake to praise your mercy
     and your glory.

6 For the hospital staff

Father,
    your Son Jesus Christ healed all kinds
        of sickness
        as he went among the crowds
            proclaiming the gospel of
                your kingdom.

Take all that is done in this hospital
    in medical and nursing care,
    in training and research,
    in physiotherapy and psychiatry,
    and in other practical ways,
        and make it a continuation of his gracious
            ministry among us.

May the members of the staff,
    whom you have equipped for this work,
come to know Jesus as their only Doctor
    and Saviour.
    I ask this in his name.

7   At night in the ward

Lord, you have compassion on the sick
   and you work by your Spirit through those
who care for them.

Have mercy on all who cannot sleep tonight
   because of their anxieties or their pain.
Bring them your healing comfort
   to body, mind and spirit.

Be with those in charge of the wards,
   with doctors and other members of the staff.
   with those on duty in the
     casualty department,
    in the ambulance stations,
      in the telephone exchange,
      and elsewhere tonight.

I pray especially for those who are nervous
   because they are inexperienced.
Equip them with all that is necessary
   from your infinite wisdom and strength
     to be agents of your grace, through
      Jesus Christ.

8   Sleeplessness

Be with me, merciful God,
  as I lie awake through this long night.

May your Holy Spirit take my soreness
  and bind me to your Son,
    who suffered for my sins
      and for those of the whole world.

May his healing and saving power
  take away my discomfort
    and establish me in his peace.
And may I rest in your love and righteousness,
  knowing that in him I am your child.

Bring me, Father, the gift of sleep,
  and may I wake in the morning refreshed
    and renewed
      because you have watched over me
        and healed me as I slept.

Through Jesus Christ I offer my prayer.

9   Discharged from hospital

My Lord and my God,
   you are present everywhere.

Look down in your love
   on the patients I am leaving here,
      especially those I have met in the ward.

I thank you for the skill and care of the staff.
Renew them as they welcome the new patients
   who are admitted today.

When I return home
   help me to accept the changes as well
      as the joys.
Prepare me, my family and my friends
   for our reunion.

Bind us together in the love of Jesus Christ,
   and through the Holy Spirit
      teach us to serve you
         in our church
            and in our neighbourhood,
              to your praise and glory.

10 Alone at home

Thank you, Jesus, my Lord and my God,
   for bringing me safely home again.
I praise you for your healing grace
   poured upon me while I was in hospital.

In your loving mercy, continue
that healing work
   during the next few days
as I settle down to my life
   within and beyond these walls.

Give me confidence to rely on your strength
   now I have to do things for myself.
Help me to welcome callers and
to greet neighbours
   in your joy and in your love.

And fill me with a spirit of praise,
   that in the company of the heavenly host
I may worship the almighty and loving Father,
   united with you here in my home.

PART 3

FOR INNER HEALING

The healing which Jesus brings is more than the cure of a disease or the removal of a disability. Often he wants us to confess our sins to him, to put right our relationships with others, and to renounce any evil influence that we may have surrendered to in the past.

Sometimes this involves seeking the help of fellow Christians, in an informal chat, in a counselling session, or in making a formal confession before a minister.

Christ is concerned with the whole of our personality. It is only when our thoughts, emotions, intentions, relationships with others – all the things which make up our lives – are under the control of his Spirit that we are able to receive his healing and know his peace.

Self-examination

Father in heaven,
   enlighten me with your Holy Spirit,
   that I may discern the sins
     which mar your image in me.

Give me the grace of humility
     to repent and confess my faults
   that I may be cleansed
     through the sacrifice of your Son,
     Jesus Christ, my Saviour and Lord.

2   **Inner healing**

Lord, I am crushed by this sense
   of my unworthiness;
     there is nothing in my life that I
       can call good.

I despise myself.
   I loathe my thoughts and desires;
     they poison and corrupt me.
If others could look into my heart
   they would never want to know me again.

But you know me, Lord, intimately.
   In your incarnate life
you saw into the hearts of women and men;
   you discerned their secret faults.
There is nothing in me that is hidden from you.

Yet you still love me,
   for you came to call sinners like me.
You are my Redeemer.

Lord, in your love, send cleansing fire into
   my innermost being.
Drive from me the spirits of self-hatred
   and depression;
     banish them so that they never trouble
      me again.
And fill me with your Spirit
   that I may grow in love for you
     and for others.

3   Repentance

God of all glory and power,
    you created me in your image,
        and wonderfully re-created me
    through the life, death, resurrection
    and ascension of your Son.

Forgive my sins which separate me from you.
Stir my heart and mind to true repentance.
Renew in me the faith which comes from you.

And send your Holy Spirit upon me
    that I may be forgiven and healed,
        and in his power joyfully praise you,
    and serve you for the purposes
        of your kingdom.

I ask this in the name of Jesus Christ.

4 Confession

Merciful Father,
I repent of my sins,
    especially . . . .

For these,
    and for all other sins which
        I cannot remember,
I am truly sorry.

I resolve not to sin again.

And I ask you, my Father, to forgive me,
    through the redemption
which your dear Son has won for me
        by his cross and resurrection.

Drive away everything which paralyses me
    and prevents me walking in your ways –
        evil thoughts,
        sinful impulses,
        depressions and anxieties,
        tensions within myself,
    and between me and others.

Send your liberating Spirit
    that I may be freed from them for ever,
    and walk in your light for ever.

5 Rejection of sin

Lord Jesus Christ,
   nailed to the cross to free me from sin,
I am ashamed and sorry that this sin
   of . . . . (1)
   persists in me.
I have been weak and selfish and proud.
I have not allowed you to rule over
   this part of my life.
I have refused your forgiveness and
   your healing power.
Forgive my stubborn will,
   break my foolish heart,
and grant me a vision and a longing
   to be freed for ever from it.
May that seed of the Holy Spirit
   which will grow into the opposite virtue
    be sown in me.
Then, by your grace, I may become
   more . . . . (2)
And as your goodness overcomes
   my sinfulness
make your throne in me,
my Sovereign Lord and Saviour.

(1) *Mention here the sins which trouble you*
    most at this moment.
(2) *Mention here the virtues or fruit of the*
    Spirit which are the opposites of those
    sins.

6   Forgiveness

Holy Father,
   in your love you sent your Son to
     be my Saviour.
He was pierced for my transgressions
   and crushed for my iniquities.
Through his stripes I am healed.

Fill me with your Holy Spirit
   that I may receive your healing
     in body, mind and spirit.

I long to be a disciple who praises
   and serves you,
   that others may turn to you
     for forgiveness, healing and faith.

Grant this prayer, Father,
   through your Son, my Redeemer.

7 Guidance

Lord God, you are the eternal Rock,
   I trust in your word
      that you will lead me in the
         path of righteousness.

You know my hesitations and my lack of faith.
   I cannot be sure of my own judgment
      when I claim healing in your name.

Guard me from error,
protect me from the effects of my
   pride and ambition,
and teach me to humble myself as a little child.

Through the power of the cross,
   pour out on me your Holy Spirit
      with gifts of discernment and wisdom.

And in the name of Jesus Christ
   I ask you to heal me, Lord,
      that with your people I may praise you
         and proclaim your love and greatness.

8   Faith

Father, your word tells us
   that faith is being sure of what we hope for
     and certain of what we do not see.

Fill me with a firm hope in your promises
   and a living faith in your power.

Work your healing in me, living God,
   that I may be whole
     in body, mind and spirit,
   to praise you and serve you
     all my life.

I ask this through Jesus Christ,
   your Son, my Saviour.

9 Truth

Spirit of God,
   hold me so that I may continue in the word
      of the Son.
Then may I truly be his disciple;
   and I will know the truth,
   and the truth will make me free:
      free from resentment and bitterness;
      free from the fear of others
         and of what they might think of me;
      free from the shadows of past experiences,
         of old and hurtful relationships;
      free to ask for a gift of repentance,
         that I might be forgiven and healed.

Spirit of holiness,
   work in me so that in Christ I may become
      a new creation.
In him, the old has gone, the new has come,
   for your work transforms us
      making us more like him.

Spirit of truth,
   reveal to me more and more
      truth about myself.
Then I may be free to serve you,
   with the Father and the Son,
      and to honour your holy Name.

10 Joy

Lord, you have revealed your word,
   that your joy may be in me.

Help me to fix my eyes upon you,
   the author and perfector of our faith,
who for the joy that was set before you
   endured the cross, despising its shame,
and who is now seated at the right hand of the
   throne of God.

In your name I ask that you will fulfil
   your purposes in me,
      whatever they may be.

Give me the faith and strength to embrace
   your purposes gladly
   that my joy may be complete,
      ascending in heart and mind to
         where you reign.

PART 4

PERSONAL SITUATIONS

In a book like this it is obviously impossible to envisage every situation in which we might find ourselves. It might be an alarming diagnosis, an accident, a disability, a convalescence, a difficult relationship with another – anything which creates a personal crisis in our lives.

We believe we are united with Jesus Christ in his passion, death, resurrection and ascension. Therefore we can wait for him to lead us through these situations and transform them with his victory. Throughout the ages Christians facing crises in their lives have discovered as never before the upholding power of his Spirit.

In this confidence we pray from the midst of our situation – and beyond it, for the fulfilment of God's purposes in us and around us. These prayers are only examples of the sorts of things we might be led to say to the Lord.

PERSONAL SITUATIONS

1 Diagnosis

Lord, I feared that it might be this.
  I shrink from what the doctor has told me.
    I'm scared of what might happen.

Yet I know that you are my salvation.
I can trust in you and not be afraid.

You are with me,
  nothing can take me out of your hand.
You are my strength.

Therefore I will sing your praises,
  and I will accept this diagnosis,
    knowing that in all things you work
  for the good of those who love you.

Fill me with your Spirit
  that I may love you more,
  and that your good purposes
  may be fulfilled in me.

2   Disease

I feel this disease gripping me
   like an evil claw, Lord Jesus.
The pain does not leave me for long;
   the drugs muddle my mind.

But I know that in your name
   there is release and healing.

I reach out in faith
   to touch the hem of your clothing.

Turn to me, Lord,
   and may the power of your Holy Spirit
cleanse me and make me whole.

I ask this for your Father's glory.

3   Accident

I praise you, loving Father,
   because your hand shielded me
     in this accident.
The awfulness of it –
   the shock, the pain, the fear, the
     sense of outrage –
     overwhelmed me.

Yet in the midst of it I called upon you,
   and you answered me.

In Jesus' name comfort those who
   were involved,
and forgive whoever was at fault.

Guide me through the consequences
   of this accident.
Heal my body,
   deliver me from resentment,
     and free me from emotional after-effects,
      by the outpouring of your loving Spirit.

4   Disabled

Jesus, our Lord and Shepherd,
   you had compassion on the weak
      and disabled,
      the two blind beggars,
      the cripple at Bethesda,
      the deaf, the dumb,
      the mentally ill,
   and those troubled by evil spirits.

I ask you in your mercy
   to grant to me your comfort and peace.
By the anointing of your Spirit
   may I have patience to accept what
      cannot be changed,
and faith to receive the healing you offer me
   in body, mind and spirit.

Equip me with discernment and love
   to respond to you in joy and thanksgiving,
      to the honour and glory of the
         heavenly Father.

5 Arthritic and elderly

Creator of the universe, Father of us all,
    everything came into existence
        through your word.
You made the heavens, even the
    highest heavens,
    and all their starry host.
Among the galaxies this planet is a speck of
    dust under your feet.

But my world lies within these four walls.
Beyond my window is a society
    which becomes stranger
    every month, every year,
    as I shuffle from bed to chair,
        from chair to table,
        from table to toilet,
    and then back to bed again.

Jesus, you are for ever united with
    our frail humanity.
Strengthen me by your Spirit to grow in faith
    and to know your presence every day.
May my shuffles be my pilgrimage
    as I seek your kingdom.
May my aches bring me to your cross.
And may I know the healing power
    of your resurrection and your glory
    here in my little space,
    that my room may be your temple
where I can praise you always.

6   Fear of death

All praise to you, Father in heaven,
   nothing can separate me from the
      love of Christ.
Whether I live or die, I am yours.

When I walk through the valley of the
   shadow of death
   I will fear no evil, for you are with me.

I come beneath the cross of your beloved Son,
   and ask you, in your mercy,
      to forgive my sins.

Prepare me, Father, to rejoice with your
   people in Zion,
      where there is no mourning nor crying
         nor any more pain.

May your Holy Spirit,
   who raised Jesus from the dead,
   raise me to healing and salvation
      to praise you in eternity.

7 Bereavement

God of all mercy,
  in your love for us you sent your Son
to break the bonds of sin and death
to invite us to share with him
  the joy and glory of his resurrection.

Show us your compassion
  as we mourn the death of N . . . .

Thank you for bringing him/her
  from the darkness of this world
    into the glorious light of your kingdom.

Help me to surrender N . . . .
  into your Fatherly care.

And through the renewing grace of your Spirit
  prepare me and all who mourn
    for the day when we are reunited
  with our brothers and sisters in Christ,
and when every tear will be wiped away.

I ask this through Jesus our Lord.

8   Convalescence

Creator and Ruler of heaven and earth,
   the universe is in the palm of your hand.

You sent your Son to give us life,
   life in all its fulness,
      living water,
      bread eternal,

Enable me to live as you willed
   in the beginning,
   washed in him,
      fed by him,
that I may enter into that wholeness
   and salvation
   which comes from you.

Give me patience during this convalescence,
   to await your guidance and your healing.

In your goodness, Lord God, hear me
   through our Saviour Jesus Christ.

9   Relationships

Jesus, our Saviour,
  your apostle instructs us
    to live at peace with everyone.

You know my relationships are in a mess.
  There are those I disagree with,
    those I dislike,
  and those I never want to see again.

Show what needs to be changed in me
  for me to embrace them in love.

Send your spirit of repentance
  so I may confess my faults;
your spirit of power
  so I may be changed;
and your spirit of love
  so I may be loving towards them.

May we follow you together,
  and with one heart and mouth
    glorify the heavenly Father.

10 Intercession

Thank you, Lord, for my friends,
   who carry me by their prayers
      into your presence.

Bless them for their faithfulness to you
   and their care for me.

May I never be weary of interceding
   for them,
   for those in need,
   for those who do not know how to
      seek your salvation.

PART 5

FOR OTHERS

Praying for others who are ill, especially when we are sick ourselves, is a particularly Christ-like ministry. When we intercede in these circumstances, we put the needs of others to God before our own, as our Lord did on the cross.

It is also a ministry of compassion ('suffering with' others). Because we are experiencing a personal crisis ourselves, we can stand alongside them and understand their particular needs better than someone enjoying good health.

1 Sick

Lord God, our Creator and Redeemer,
  you sent your Son as the light
    of the world
  to open the eyes of those in darkness,
  to give hearing to the deaf,
  to free the tongues of the dumb,
and to restore withered limbs.

Have mercy on the sick.
Meet them in their various needs,
Heal their weaknesses and infirmities,
  so that, knowing your power
    within themselves,
they may rejoice in your mercy
  and follow in the way of Jesus.

We ask this in his name.

2   Paralysed

Jesus, those four men brought
　　　their friend to you
　and lowered him to your feet
　　　on a stretcher.

We bring before you those
　　　who are paralysed,
　in mind and emotions as well as
　　　in body,
　　　　through accidents and injustices
　and through mental and
　　　physical disorders.

Look on them in compassion,
　　　forgive them their sins,
　　　　and command them to rise and walk.

So may they continue their lives,
　　　rejoicing in your goodness
　and telling men and women everywhere
　　　the good news of the Father's
　　　　unfailing love.

3 Crippled

Holy Spirit of God,
bring your healing gifts
to mend the lives of those
   crippled in body or mind.

May the balm of your anointing
   flow over them,
     giving them your peace
and restoring their weakened limbs.

Strengthen them so that they may
   keep in step with you,
     lifting hands to our heavenly Father
and praising the name of Jesus Christ
      our Saviour,
who through your empowering
   released the lame to leap for joy.

4   Bedridden

We remember before you, Lord,
   all those who are confined
      to their beds
   at home or in nursing establishments.

Be with them in their loneliness,
   take away their despair
   and fill them with hope in you.

Bless those who care for them;
   enable them to be patient
      with one another.

Bring them visitors from among
   their relatives and friends
   and equip your church to
      minister to them.

In the name of Jesus Christ
   we ask this.

5 Those in pain

Breathe your spirit of healing,
    Lord Jesus,
    on all those who are in pain.
Banish any bitterness or
    anxiety from them.

Fill them with the graces of patience,
    endurance and hope.

Relieve them of all discomfort,
    bring them your peace,
        and give them confidence and trust
            in our heavenly Father,
        through the overshadowing of
            your Holy Spirit.

6 Alcoholics, smokers and drug addicts

Gracious Lord,
   the helper of all who trust in you,
we pray particularly for those
   who are addicted to alcohol,
      tobacco and drugs.

Give them both the desire and the will
   to be freed from their slavery,
and pour upon them your grace
   and guidance,
      leading them to your liberty
      and salvation.

Grant us the patience and love
   to stand by them
      in compassion and encouragement
   as servants of your hope and strength.

Lord, hear us for them.

7   Mentally ill

Holy Spirit,
   you search out all things,
the deep things of God
   and the deep things of women and men.

We ask you to penetrate
   into the inner depths
of those who are sick in mind.

Give them your cleansing,
   your healing, your wholeness.

Sanctify their memories,
   cast out their fears,
and inspire them to love you
   with new hearts and minds.

Then will they glorify the Father
   through the Son
      in your power.

8 Those losing hope

All merciful God,
your consolation never fails us.
    You comfort us in all our troubles.

Come in your love
to those who are losing hope,
    who despair of ever being well again.

May they know your presence and power,
    so that they too can comfort others
with the consolation
        they receive from you.

In the name of Jesus Christ,
    whom you sent as our Redeemer
        and Healer,
        we ask this, our Father.

9   Those who are dangerously ill

Lord Jesus, enthroned in glory,
   you are the Alpha and the Omega,
   the Beginning and the End.
You clothe us with healing
    and salvation
   in your eternity.

Stretch out your merciful hand
   upon those who are dangerously ill.

Pour on them your refreshing grace
   from the spring of the water of life.

Release them from fear,
   give them faith and hope in you,
and bestow on them
   your peace and healing.

So will the Father be their
   only delight,
   and you their Saviour and King,
    in the love and power of the
    Holy Spirit.

10   Those believed to be incurable

Father God,
we pray for those who are suffering
    from diseases for which at present
        there is no known cure.

Give them victory over their fears
    and trust in your love.

Grant wisdom to all who research
    to discover cures for
        these diseases.

And in the name of your Son,
        Jesus Christ,
    who is our health and salvation,
we ask you in your mercy to make
        them well again
    by gifts of your Holy Spirit,
        to your glory.

PART 6

MORNING AND EVENING PRAYERS

We are not able to concentrate for long on our prayers when we are ill. Even handling a Bible can be too much of an effort. This part draws together scriptural material and prayers for a brief act of devotion in the morning and the evening of each day during one week.

They consist of the following:

Morning Prayers:

An act of praise using a verse of Scripture, with which to recollect the presence of God.

A Bible passage of three or four verses, followed by a few comments. Ignore these comments if they are not helpful and concentrate for a short time on the passage.

A prayer based on thoughts arising
from the passage.

An act of thanksgiving. What is
included in this will, of course,
depend on individual circumstances.

Topics for intercession for the Church
and for the world.

A saying of Jesus to memorise and
recall during the day.

Evening Prayers:

An act of penitence with
accompanying scriptural verses. A
form of confession is printed on
page 40.

A psalm.

A space for personal intercessions.

Two or three verses of a hymn.

A traditional prayer for the end
of the day.

Sunday Morning

*Praise be to the God and Father of our Lord Jesus
Christ! In his great mercy he has given us new birth
into a living hope through the resurrection of Jesus
Christ from the dead!*   1 Peter 1.3

Reading: Luke 24:30–32

> When Jesus was at table with them, he took bread,
> gave thanks, broke it and began to give it to them.
> Then their eyes were opened and they recognised
> him, and he disappeared from their sight. They
> asked each other, 'Were not our hearts burning
> within us while he talked with us on the road and
> opened the Scriptures to us?'

The risen Christ made himself known to his
disciples as he said the prayer of thanksgiving over
the bread. It was a very ordinary thing to do. All
devout Jews gave thanks before a meal. But it was
during that ordinary action that the wonderful truth
of the resurrection was revealed to the disciples.
And, when Jesus disappeared from their sight, they
realised that while he had been speaking to them
about the Scriptures, the Holy Spirit had been stir-
ring their hearts.

The risen Christ meets us too, amidst the ordinary things of life. Often, though, we don't recog-
nise his presence until we look back afterwards on
what we have experienced. Only when we are completely open to the Spirit do we realise Jesus is in
our situation, whatever it is. 'He who has the Son
has life' (1 Jn 5.12).

Prayer

Father God, teach me to know
  your risen Son
  in the midst of everything
    I experience.
I pray that I may realise his presence
  especially during the difficult days
    of this illness.
Send your Holy Spirit upon me
  that he may take away my doubts,
    fears and weaknesses,
  and set me on fire with faith,
    hope and love.
I rest upon you and upon your word.
I ask this through the death and
  resurrection of Jesus,
  who unites me to you by the
    same Spirit.

Lord, I thank you for . . .

I pray for my church and all Christian
  congregations everywhere
  –for those who are facing
  persecutions in other lands
      –for those who proclaim your
        Gospel and teach your people
      –for those who are to be
        baptised and confirmed today.

A WORD FOR TODAY

Jesus said: *'Surely I am with you always, to the very
end of the age.'*   Mt 28.20

Sunday Evening

Confession

> *The sacrifice of God is a broken spirit: a*
> *broken and contrite heart he will not*
> *despise.*   Psalm 51.15

Lord, I confess . . .

> *Jesus said, 'This is my blood of the*
> *covenant, which is poured out for many for the*
> *forgiveness of sins.'*   Matthew 26.28

Psalm 134

1   Come, bless the Lord, all you
      servants of the Lord:
    you that by night stand in the house
       of our God.

2   Lift up your hands towards the holy
       place and bless the Lord:
    may the Lord bless you from Zion,
    the Lord who made heaven and earth.

    Glory to the Father and to the Son:
       and to the Holy Spirit;
    as it was in the beginning is now:
       and shall be for ever. Amen.

Intercessions

> Lord, I pray for . . .

Hymn

> Alleluia! Alleluia!
>   Hearts to heaven and voices raise;
> Sing to God a hymn of gladness,
>   Sing to God a hymn of praise:
> He who on the cross a victim
>   For the world's salvation bled,
> Jesus Christ, the King of Glory,
>   Now is risen from the dead.
>
> Christ is risen, we are risen;
>   Shed upon us heavenly grace,
> Rain, and dew, and gleams of glory
>   From the brightness of thy face;
> That we, with our hearts in heaven,
>   Here on earth may fruitful be,
> And by angel-hands be gathered,
>   And be ever, Lord, with thee.
> *Bishop Christopher Wordsworth,*   *1807–1885*

Lighten our darkness, Lord, we pray; and in your mercy defend us from all perils and dangers of this night; for the love of your only Son, our Saviour Jesus Christ.

Monday Morning

The grace of God that brings salvation has appeared to all men.   Titus 2.11

Reading: Exodus 34.29–32

> When Moses came down from Mount Sinai with the two tablets of the Testimony in his hands, he was not aware that his face was radiant because he had spoken with the Lord. When Aaron and all the Israelites saw Moses . . ., they were afraid to come near him. But Moses called to them; so Aaron and all the leaders of the community came back to him, and he spoke to them. Afterwards all the Israelites came near him, and he gave them all the commands the Lord had given him on Mount Sinai.

When we're ill, it's easy to feel sorry for ourselves. Love of neighbour can seem very secondary when we are overwhelmed by our own needs. And when we don't get better quickly, we wonder if God really loves us any more.

This Old Testament story looks forward to when Jesus Christ revealed for us God's new covenant. Accepting the new law of the Gospel, we also accept Christ as ruler over our lives and circumstances. In return, he gives us his Spirit, and in his Spirit we begin to experience 'the glorious freedom of the children of God' (Rom 8.21). Like the disciples on the mount of Transfiguration, we see our relationship with Jesus in God's light. Our attention is focused on him instead of on ourselves. The illness—at home, in hospital—can be an important step in our own spiritual journey up the mount of Christian discipleship.

Prayer

Sovereign Lord of my life,
   I praise you for the light and freedom
     you offer people through your
     law of love.
Write that law on the pages
   of my heart,
   so I may know your glorious presence
     and enter into your liberty.
May I be changed into the likeness
   of your Son, Jesus Christ,
     with ever-increasing glory by
     your Spirit
   to the praise of your holy name.

Lord, I thank you for . . .

I pray for our nation and those in
   authority in it
   –for racial harmony and
    social justice
   –for peace in the world
   –for the European Council
    and the United Nations.

A WORD FOR TODAY

Jesus said: *'You did not choose me, but I chose you.'* (Jn 15.16)

Monday Evening

Confession

*Wash me thoroughly from my wickedness: and
cleanse me from my sin.*   Psalm 51.2

Lord, I confess . . .

*God demonstrates his love for us in this: While
we were still sinners, Christ died for us.*
                                        Romans 5.8

Psalm 119.33–35

Teach me, O Lord, to follow
    your decrees;
    then I will keep them to the end.

Give me understanding, and I will
    keep your law
    and obey it with all my heart.

Direct me in the path of your commands,
    for there I find delight.

Glory to the Father, and to the Son,
    and to the Holy Spirit;
as it was in the beginning, is now,
    and shall be for ever.

Intercessions

> Lord, I pray for . . .

Hymn

> The day thou gavest, Lord, is ended,
>   The darkness falls at thy behest;
> To thee our morning hymns ascended,
>   Thy praise shall sanctify our rest.
>
> The sun that bids us rest is waking
>   Our brethren 'neath the western sky,
> And hour by hour fresh lips are making
>   Thy wondrous doings heard on high.
>
> So be it, Lord; thy throne shall never,
>   Like earth's proud empires, pass away;
> Thy Kingdom stands, and grows for ever,
>   Till all thy creatures own thy sway.
>   *J. Ellerton, 1826–93*

Visit this home (hospital), Lord, we pray;
drive far from it all the snares of the evil one;
may your holy angels dwell with us and
guard us in peace; and may your blessing
be always upon us, through Jesus Christ
our Lord.

Tuesday Morning

Worthy is the Lamb, who was slain, to receive power and wealth and wisdom and strength and honour and glory and praise.　　　　　　Revelation 5.12

Reading: 1 John 3.1,2

> How great is the love the Father has lavished on us, that we should be called children of God! And that is what we are! The reason the world does not know us is that it did not know him. Dear friends, now we are children of God, and what we will be has not yet been made known. But we know that when it is made known, we shall be like him, for we shall see him as he is.

Everyone is either a child of God, or potentially a child of God. With some people, because they have accepted the faith of Jesus Christ, that relationship with the Father is growing. With others, who are searching for him, that relationship has not yet developed. Even those who seem to reject God may well have an unacknowledged hunger for him in their hearts. 'From everlasting to everlasting God's love is with those who fear him, and his righteousness with their children's children' (Ps 106.1).

Whoever we meet, then, falls into one or other of these categories. This applies when we are ill at home or in hospital. And, as God's children ourselves, we are his ministers to those who come to serve us. Even in the briefest encounters with folk like doctors and nurses, we are to reflect the love of our Father and the compassion of Jesus, who is their Saviour and Friend as well as ours.

Prayer

Heavenly Father,
   you have claimed me as your child
      and in Jesus given me a Friend
      as my Saviour.
Help me to treat all those I meet
   as your children and his friends.
Lead us all into the fortress of
   your salvation,
      and use me as one of your servants
      for them.

Lord, I thank you for . . .

I pray for those at work
–for those in education, research
 and social service
–for those who maintain the
 life of the community
–for the unemployed and those
 victimised at work.

A WORD FOR TODAY

Jesus said: *'My command is this: Love one another
as I have loved you.'*   Jn 15.13, 14.

Tuesday Evening

Confession

> *Create in me a clean heart O God: and renew a
> right spirit within me.*   Psalm 51.10

Lord, I confess . . .

> *Christ died for all, that those who lived should
> no longer live for themselves but for him who
> died for them and was raised again.*
>   1 Corinthians 5.15

Psalm 28.6–9

Praise be to the Lord,
  for he has heard my cry for mercy.
The Lord is my strength and my shield;
  my heart trusts in him, and I am helped.
My heart leaps for joy
  and I will give thanks to him in song.
The Lord is the strength of his people,
  a fortress of salvation for his
    anointed one.
Save your people and bless your
  inheritance;
  be their shepherd and carry them
    for ever.
Glory to the Father, and to the Son,
  and to the Holy Spirit;
as it was in the beginning, is now,
  and shall be for ever.

Intercessions

> Lord, I pray for . . .

Hymn

> O thou who camest from above
>   The pure celestial fire to impart,
> Kindle a flame of sacred love
>   On the mean altar of my heart.
>
> There let it for thy glory burn
>   With inextinguishable blaze,
> And trembling to its source return
>   In humble prayer and fervent praise.
>
> Jesus, confirm my heart's desire,
>   To work and speak and think for thee;
> Still let me guard the holy fire
>   And still stir up thy gift in me.
>
> Still let me prove thy perfect will,
>   My acts of faith and love repeat;
> Till death thy endless mercies seal,
>   And make the sacrifice complete.
>   *Charles Wesley, 1707–1788*

Look down, O Lord from your throne in heaven,
let the light of your presence dispel the shadows of
the night; and from the children of light banish the
deeds of darkness; through Jesus Christ our Lord.

Wednesday Morning

*By day and night the four living creatures round the
throne never stop singing, Holy, holy, holy is the
Lord God Almighty, who was, and is, and is to
come.*   Revelation 4.8

Reading: Acts 16.9–10

> During the night Paul had a vision of a man of
> Macedonia standing and begging him, 'Come over
> into Macedonia and help us.' After Paul had seen
> the vision, we got ready at once to leave for
> Macedonia, concluding that God had called us to
> preach the gospel to them.

The second missionary journey of Paul took a
dramatic turn. With his companions (Timothy and
Luke—the latter including himself, 'we') the
apostle had been prevented from continuing his
work in Asia; but now from over the water came an
invitation to cross into Europe and preach the
Gospel there. With his friends he obeyed the call of
God through the man of Macedonia, and so the
Church was established in a new continent.

Frustrations are plenty when we're ill. But if we
trust God, we shall find he can use even frustrations
for his purposes. Paul wrote, 'We know that in all
things God works for the good of those who love
him, who have been called according to his purpose
(Rom 8.28). Like the apostle, we must be alert for
the vision God sends, the word he utters, the
opportunity he opens up—and then take the
initiative in obedience to him.

Prayer

> Lord, in joy I respond to your call;
>   teach me to hear your voice.
> Guide me as your servant along the road
>   of your choice.
> I offer to you the frustrations,
>   the time-wasting,
>   and the setbacks of this illness.
> May they be pavingstones in the path you
>   set before me.
>   In the power of your Spirit
>   use me in this place for the purposes
>   of your Gospel
>   and the glory of your kingdom.
> I ask for these graces in Jesus' name.

> Lord, I thank you for . . .

> I pray for the poor and underprivileged
> throughout the world
>   –for the hungry and deprived
>   –for those politically and socially oppressed
>   –for those robbed of family, home and
>   community

A WORD FOR TODAY

Jesus said: *'Do not be afraid, little flock, for your
Father has been pleased to give you the kingdom.'*

Lk 12.32–34

Wednesday Evening

Confession

> *The Lord our God is merciful and forgiving,*
> *even though we have rebelled against him.*
>
> Daniel 9.9

Lord, I confess . . .

> *We do not have a high priest who is unable to*
> *sympathise with our weaknesses, but we have*
> *one who has been tempted in every way, just as*
> *we are—yet without sin.* Hebrews 4.15

Psalm 100

Shout for joy to the Lord, all the earth.
Worship the Lord with gladness:
   come before him with joyful songs.
Know that the Lord is God.
   It is he who made us, and we are his;
we are his people, the sheep
   of his pasture.
Enter his gates with thanksgiving and
   his courts with praise;
   give thanks to him and praise his name.
For the Lord is good and his love
   endures for ever;
   his faithfulness continues through
    all generations.
Glory to the Father, and to the Son,
   and to the Holy Spirit;
as it was in the beginning, is now,
   and shall be for ever.

Intercessions

Lord, I pray for . . .

Hymn

Round me falls the night;
Saviour, be my light:
Through the hours in
   darkness shrouded
Let me see thy face
   unclouded;
Let thy glory shine
In this heart of mine.

Earthly work is done,
Earthly sounds are none;
Rest in sleep and silence
   seeking,
Let me hear thee softly
   speaking;
In my spirit's ear
Whisper, 'I am near.'

Blessed, heavenly Light,
Shining through earth's night;
Voice, that oft of love has told me;
Arms, so strong to clasp and hold me;
Thou thy watch wilt keep,
Saviour, o'er my sleep.

W. Romanis, 1824–1899

Be with us, merciful God, and protect us through
the silent hours of this night; that we, who are
wearied by the changes and chances of this fleeting
world, may rest upon your eternal changelessness;
through Jesus Christ our Lord.

Thursday Morning

To the only God our Saviour be glory, majesty, power and authority, through Jesus Christ our Lord, before all ages, now and for evermore. Jude 25

Reading: Isaiah 63.7

> I will tell of the kindnesses of the Lord, the deeds for which he is to be praised, according to all the Lord has done for us—yes, the many good things he has done for the house of Israel, according to his compassion and many kindnesses.

I look back over my life and recall the many good things God has done for me and for my 'house' (family). For creating me and giving me an opportunity of enjoying this life; through it I have seen the beauty of the Life-Giver. For parents and others who looked after me; they reflected the compassion and love of my Redeemer. For those who spent time and care teaching me and encouraging my abilities; it was they who were instruments of the wisdom and purpose of God.

Especially I recall those who, through the Holy Spirit, revealed to me the Gospel of the kingdom of God. Those who taught me his word and, by the way they lived, pointed me to the Lord. There is so much from God for me to treasure. 'Guard the good deposit that was entrusted to you—guard it with the help of the Holy Spirit who lives in us' (2 Tim 1.14).

Prayer

Lord God, you are always to be praised,
  for the many good deeds you have
    done in my life,
for the redemption you offer me
  through your Son, Jesus Christ,
and for the outpouring of your Holy Spirit,
  who brings me into the company of
    your faithful people.
I thank you for the compassion and
  kindnesses you show me now,
  in the midst of this illness.

May I receive your Spirit anew this day
  to be strengthened and healed, and
to love, worship and serve you all my days.

I pray for my family and my friends
–for my neighbours and acquaintances
–for those who are going through difficult
    times
–for those who are estranged from one another

A WORD FOR TODAY

*Jesus said: 'Ask and it will be given to you; seek and
you will find; knock and the door will be opened to
you.'* Mt 7.7,8

Thursday Evening

Confession

> *You that fear the Lord trust in the Lord: he is
> your help and your shield.* Psalm 115.10

Lord, I confess . . .

> *For God so loved the world that he gave his one
> and only Son, that whoever believes in him
> shall not perish but have eternal life.* John 3.16

Psalm 116. 1, 2, 12, 14

> I love the Lord, for he heard my voice;
>   he heard my cry for mercy.
> Because he turned his ear to me,
>   I will call upon him as long as I live.
> How can I repay the Lord,
>   for all his goodness to me?
> I will fulfil my vows to the Lord,
>   in the presence of all his people.
> Glory to the Father, and to the Son,
>   and to the Holy Spirit;
> as it was in the beginning, is now,
>   and shall be for ever.

Intercessions

　　Lord, I pray for . . .

Hymn

Come, thou Holy Spirit,
　come,
And from thy celestial
　home
　　Shed a ray of light
　　divine;
Come, thou Father of the
　poor,
Come, thou source of all
　our store,
　　Come, within our
　　bosoms shine:

Heal our wounds; our
　strength renew;
On our dryness pour
　thy dew;
Wash the stains of guilt
　away;
Bend the stubborn
　heart and will;
Melt the frozen, warm
　the chill;
Guide the steps that go
　astray.

　　On the faithful who adore
　　And confess thee, evermore
　　In thy sevenfold gifts descend:
　　Give them virtue's sure reward,
　　Give them thy salvation, Lord,
　　Give them joys that never end.
　　　　Archbishop Stephen Langton, d. 1228

Lord, support us all the day long of this troublous
life, until the shades lengthen, and the evening
comes, and the busy world is hushed, the fever of
life is over, and our work is done. Then, Lord, in
your mercy grant us safe lodging, a holy rest, and
peace at the last; through Jesus Christ our Lord.

Friday Morning

*May I never boast except in the cross of our Lord
Jesus Christ, through whom the world has been
crucified to me, and I to the world.*

Galatians 6.14

Reading: Romans 8.35–37

> Who shall separate us from the love of Christ?
> Shall trouble or hardship or persecution or famine
> or nakedness or danger or sword? As it is written:
> 'For your sake we face death all day long;
> we are to be considered as sheep to be
> slaughtered.'
> No, in all these things we are more than conquerors
> through him who loved us.

Paul endured many things as an apostle of Jesus
Christ—floggings, exposed to death on numerous
occasions, stoned, shipwrecked three times, twenty
four hours in the open sea, in danger of bandits and
opponents, hungry, thirsty, cold, weighed down by
responsibilities (2 Cor 11.29). No wonder he
quoted the psalmist (44.22) who complained to
God that he felt no better than a sheep being led to
the slaughterhouse!

But the apostle knew that God in his love had
sent his Son into the sufferings of this world, and
that through the cross Jesus had won a victory in
which we can all share. The secret lies in total trust
and dependence on him. Nothing—no sickness, no
treatment, no diagnosis, no experience, not even
death itself—is to be feared as an enemy. He is
victor over them all. We, too, can be more than
conquerors.

Prayer

> You know, Lord, how my heart shrinks
>> from thoughts of pain and disability.
> Inwardly I am a complete coward:
>> I would rather do anything than
>>> have to suffer.
> But your word exhorts me to trust in your love.
>> Send your Holy Spirit, Father,
>>> as you sent him on your Son
>>>> for our salvation.
> Shield me so that in all that I have to face
>> I am more than a conqueror.
>>> Lift me up to praise your glory

Lord, I thank you for . . .

I pray for those who suffer in body,
  mind and spirit
  –for those who are victims of famine,
  drought, and natural disasters.
  –for those who are refugees, persecuted, or
  in prison
  –for those exercising ministries of care and
  relief

A WORD FOR TODAY

Jesus said: *'If anyone would come after me, he must deny himself and take up his cross daily and follow me.'*   Lk 9.22–25

Friday Evening

Confession

> *He who dwells in the shelter of the Most High:*
> *who dwells under the shadow of the Almighty,*
> *he will say to the Lord, 'You are my refuge and*
> *my stronghold: my God in whom I trust.'*
>
> Psalm 91.1, 2

Lord, I confess . . .

> *If we confess our sins, he is faithful and just and*
> *will forgive us our sins and purify us from all*
> *unrighteousness.*
>
> 1 John 1.9

Psalm 3.1–5

> O Lord, how many are my foes!
> How many rise up against me!
> Many are saying of me,
>   'God will not deliver him'.
> But you are a shield round me, O Lord;
>   you bestow glory on me and lift up my head.
> To the Lord I cry aloud,
>   and he answers me from his holy hill.
> I lie down and sleep:
>   I wake again because the Lord sustains me.
> Glory to the Father, and to the Son, and to
>   the Holy Spirit;
> as it was in the beginning, is now,
>   and shall be for ever.

Intercessions

Lord, I pray for . . .

Hymn

> God, that madest earth and heaven,
> Darkness and light;
> Who the day for toil has given,
> For rest the night;
> May thine angel-guard defend us,
> Slumber sweet thy mercy send us,
> Holy dreams and hopes attend us,
> This livelong night.
>
> Guard us waking, guard us sleeping,
> And, when we die,
> May we in thy mighty keeping
> All peaceful lie:
> When the last dread call shall wake us,
> Do not thou our God forsake us,
> But to reign in glory take us
> With thee on high.

Bishop R. Heber, 1783–1826
Archbishop Whately, 1787–1863

Remember, O Lord, what you have worked in us, not what we deserve; and as you have called us to your service, make us worthy of our calling; through Jesus Christ our Lord.

Saturday Morning

*Let us love one another, for love comes from God.
Everyone who loves has been born of God and
knows God.*   1 John 4.7

Reading: Matthew 8.2–4

> A man with leprosy came and knelt before him,
> and said, 'Lord, if you are willing, you can make
> me clean.' Jesus reached out his hand and touched
> the man. I am willing,' he said. 'Be clean!'
> Immediately he was cured of his leprosy. Then
> Jesus said to him, 'See that you don't tell
> anyone. But go, show yourself to the priest and
> offer the gift Moses commanded, as a testimony to
> them.'

Jesus' healing ministry was a sign of the salvation—
the wholeness—he was bringing into the world. To
call him Saviour is the same as calling him Healer.
In the Bible the healing of the body and the saving
of the person are the same great blessing of God's
new covenant.

Jesus is as willing to make us well as he is willing
to forgive our sins. The trouble is that other things
—the defects of fallen humanity as well as our
personal failings—prevent him from completing
our salvation, our wholeness, in this world. We
shall find our true healing in heaven. But healing
gifts of the Holy Spirit are manifested here and now
when we ask Jesus, as the man with leprosy
discovered. Are we sometimes afraid to ask the
Lord for healing because we're not willing to face
the changes he wants to make in our lives?

Prayer

Jesus, Lord and Saviour,
   you have provided so much for us
      in the resources of nursing and medicine.
You have brought us salvation as our Healer.
Teach me, like the leper, to fall at your feet
   in complete trust,
      knowing that through your grace I
         can be healed
         and changed more into your likeness
   to praise your holy name.

Lord, I thank you for . . .

I pray for those who are tempted
   and despairing
   –for those who are sick and handicapped.
   –for the aged, the lonely, and those who
         mourn
   –for those who care for them

I remember with thankfulness those I have
known and loved who have departed this life.

A WORD FOR TODAY

Jesus said: '*I am the light of the world. Whoever
follows me will never walk in darkness, but will have
the light of life.*'   Jn 8.12

Saturday Evening

Confession

> *Teach me O Lord the way of your statutes: and
> I will honour it to the end.*   Psalm 119.33

Lord I confess . . .

> *It is by grace you have been saved, through
> faith—and this comes not from yourselves, it is
> the gift of God.*   Ephesians 2.8

Psalm 147.1–3

> Praise the Lord.
>   how good it is to sing praises
>   to our God,
>   how pleasant and fitting to praise him!
> The Lord builds up Jerusalem;
>   he gathers the exiles of Israel.
> He heals the broken-hearted
>   and binds up their wounds.
> Glory to the Father, and to the Son,
>   and to the Holy Spirit;
> as it was in the beginning, is now,
>   and shall be for ever.

Intercession

> Lord, I pray for . . .

Hymn

> At even, ere the sun was set,
> The sick, O Lord, around thee lay;
> O in what divers pains they met!
> O with what joy they went away!
>
> Thy touch has still its ancient power;
> No word from thee can fruitless fall;
> Hear, in this solemn evening hour,
> And in thy mercy heal us all.
>
> *H. Twells, 1823–1900*

May the Lord bless us and watch over us,
may the Lord make his face to shine upon us
    and be gracious to us
may the Lord look kindly upon us and
    give us peace;
and may the blessing of God almighty,
the Father, the Son, and the Holy Spirit,
be among us and remain with us always.

PART 7

OTHER PEOPLE'S PRAYERS

Christians have prayed for healing in every age. Some of their prayers are deeply personal, giving us a glimpse of their faith in God and their understanding of what he was teaching them through their illnesses and disabilities. Other prayers have a more general character; these have been adopted for use in worship and found their way into ancient or modern prayer books.

I have selected the prayers in this part from books and other sources which I have seen in the last few years. The only reason for including them here is that they have helped me in the past, and I hope they might help others, too.

1 Lord, God of mercies
   deign to stretch out thy hands,
   in thy kindness, heal all the sick,
   in thy kindness, make them worthy
      of health,
   deliver them from their present
      sickness;
   in the name of thine only-begotten Son,
   grant them recovery;
   let this holy name be a remedy
   for health and restoration.
   Through him, glory to thee and power,
   in the Holy Spirit,
   now and for ever and ever. Amen.

*From an ancient collection of prayers attributed to
Serapion, abbot of the monastery of Thumis, Egypt,
about A.D. 339.*

2 O merciful Lord,
   visit and heal this sick person,
   now lying on the bed of sickness and
      sorely afflicted,
   as thou, O Saviour, didst once raise
      Peter's wife's mother
   and the man sick of the palsy who was
      carried on his bed:
   for thou alone hast borne
   the sickness and afflictions
      of our race,
   and with thee nothing is impossible,
   for thou art all merciful.

A prayer from the liturgy of the Eastern Orthodox Churches.

3 Almighty and everlasting God,
   who canst banish all affliction
   both of soul and body;
   show forth the power of thine aid
   upon those who are sick,
   that by the help of thy mercy
   they may be restored to serve thee afresh
   in holiness of living;
   through Jesus Christ our Lord.

*From the Gelasian Sacramentary, a collection of
liturgical prayers ascribed to Gelasius, Bishop of
Rome, 492–496, but probably compiled in the seventh
or eighth century.*

4 Thou O Christ art all I want,
More than all in thee I find.
Raise the fallen, cheer the faint,
Heal the sick, and lead the blind.
Just and holy is thy name.
I am all unrighteousness.
False and full of sin I am,
Thou art full of truth and grace.

Plenteous grace with thee is found,
Grace to cover all my sin.
Let the healing streams abound,
Make and keep me pure within.
Thou of life the fountain art,
Freely let me take of thee;
Spring thou up within my heart,
Rise to all eternity.

Charles Wesley, 1707–1788

5 Lord, deliver us from all impatience and from all fear of our bodies, and fill us at the same time with spiritual fear; let us not be afraid of pain or sickness, but let us be afraid of thee and not waste the opportunity which thou art now affording us.

Give us grace to think under the visitation of light sickness whether we are fit to be visited with dangerous sickness; let us consider what we should be if, while our body were weakened, our mind should be clouded also, so that we could not then pray to thee for succour.

Now, therefore, O Lord, teach us to call on thee while we can call on thee, to think on thee while our reason is yet in its vigour. Teach us to look into our heart and life, to consider how thou wouldst judge us, to ask thy forgiveness through thy Son Jesus Christ, for all that thou seest amiss in us, and by the help of thy Holy Spirit to overcome all that is evil in our hearts, and to learn and practise all that is good.

Restore us in thy good time to our usual health, and grant that this interruption of it may be sanctified to our soul's health, so making it not an evil to us, but an infinite blessing.

Thomas Arnold, 1795–1842

6 O Almighty God,
who art the giver of all health,
and the aid of them that seek
   thee for succour;
we call upon thee for thy help
   and goodness
mercifully to be showered upon this
   thy servant,
that being healed of his infirmities,
he may give thanks to thee in thy
   holy Church;
through Jesus Christ our Lord.

*The Order for the Visitation of the Sick, The Book of
Common Prayer with the Additions and Deviations
Proposed in 1928.*

7   O Almighty God, our merciful Father,
    we pray for thy servant
    that thou wilt grant him perfect health,
    raise him up from his sickness,
    and impart to him health of body and soul;
    for thou art the Saviour and Benefactor,
    the Lord and King of all.

*The Administration of Holy Unction and the Laying
on of Hands, 1935, authorised for use in the Province
of Canterbury.*

8 O God, enrich our lives, we beseech thee, with those experiences which seem most hard to bear. Take from us all resentment and bitterness. Teach us to forgive others lest we shut ourselves from thy forgiveness. Help us to bring happiness and peace to others, even when our own hearts are in turmoil. Save us from spreading grief and sorrow, depression and despair. May we never sell our courage to buy sympathy. May we never sell another's good name to buy pity for ourselves. May we never blunt the truth about ourselves in order to excuse ourselves, or hide our motives from the scrutiny the truth warrants. Show us that it is more enriching to show courage than to receive sympathy, even when no-one suspects that there is anything to be courageous about. Show us that silent suffering, without bitterness or self-pity, can make us strong. From advertising our self-martyrdoms, from blazing abroad our little sacrifices, from reciting our woes to others, O Lord, deliver us. From yielding to melancholy moods that depress us; from the sullenness of temper that drives the sunshine from other faces; from the refusal to do battle with gloom and by that refusal to make life harder for others, O Lord, deliver us. May we be more ready to give to others our bread and our wine, than to tell them of our hunger and our thirst.

Forgive us for all our failures, and help us to start again each day as thy loving sons and daughters, living in obedience and in trust. Through Jesus Christ our Lord.

Leslie D. Weatherhead (1893–1975), Methodist minister of the City Temple, London, and author of many books.

9 By the bruising of my whole life,
    strengthen me with sympathy for every
      wounded soul,
and let my prayers be as balm for
    the wounds of
    thy children,
    that they may be healed.

*Dorothy Kerin (1889–1963), founder of the
Burrswood Home of Healing.*

10 Lord Jesus, you know what pain is like.
You know
the torture of the scourge upon your back,
the sting of the thorns upon your brow,
the agony of the nails in your hands.
You know what I'm going through just now.
Help me
to bear my pain
gallantly, cheerfully and patiently.
And help me to remember
that I will never be tried
above what I am able to bear,
and that you are with me,
even in this valley of the deep dark shadow.
In ev'ry pang that rends the heart,
the Man of Sorrows had a part;
he sympathises with our grief,
and to the suff'rer sends relief.

*William Barclay, 1907–1978, a Scottish New
Testament scholar and author of over 60 books,
many of them bestsellers; he was afflicted with
deafness for most of his life.*

11 We who stand in the world offer ourselves and
      our society for your blessed healing.
    We confess we have failed to love as you did.
    We have been socially unjust, and our
      society is imperfect,
        fragmented, and sometimes sick to death.
    Teach us your ways in the world and in this life
      which we share together.
    Don't let us restrict you to a narrow ghetto
      labelled 'religion',
    but lead us to worship you in the fulness of life
      as the lord of politics, economics
      and the arts.
    Give us light to see true morality, not in narrow
      legalisms but in sacrifices and
      open responsibility.
    Show us how to express our love for you in
      very specific, human service to other men.
    Lord, change our hearts from hearts of stone
      to hearts of flesh, and let us give thanks to
      you for all of life.

Malcolm Boyd, an American Episcopal priest.

12   The worst of pain, O Lord,
is that it makes it difficult to pray.
Yet, O Lord, I desire to pray,
to have communion with you,
to draw strength and healing from you,
to link to you those I love
and those who need your love,
to thank you for those who look after me,
and those who wish me well.

George Appleton, formerly Anglican Archbishop in Jerusalem.

13 Loving Father, we praise your name that you have drawn close to us in Jesus Christ and revealed what you have provided for us and want us to have from your hand. Thank you for your promise to us that the prayer of faith will enable the sick person to be restored to health.

We praise you that you have also revealed to us how we are to pray. Father, forgive us that so very often we have not prayed in the way that Jesus taught us. We would repent of that, and by your grace, so pray that your blessing may be given to us now and at all times.

Father God, I now accept your healing for my need. I accept it humbly and gratefully and completely. I accept it so that it is what I accept and the way I think of myself. I thank you for it and rejoice that I am giving glory to you by exercising faith. I thank you now and will continue to thank you until faith gives way to sight.

Show me what I can do to put my faith into action. As my faith is small, I know you will not expect me to act upon my faith all at once, but I believe you are showing me the first step I am to take. Through Christ our Lord.

Jim Glennon, an Australian Anglican priest.

14 Lord Jesus Christ
come through the locked doors of our lives
and stand in our area of fear,
speak your word of peace,
show us your wounds in which are our healing,
breathe anew your Holy Spirit upon us;
that filled with his perfect love and
    freed from fear,
we may obey your sending,
and go with new power and authority to
    heal your world.

*John Richards, an Anglican priest who is the
director of Renewal Servicing.*

15 Holy God and Father of all,
you who are the source of health and healing,
you who relieve suffering and
    comfort the afflicted,
have mercy on me and my loved ones.
Rescue us from all sickness.
Restore us to that health and vigour which is in
    accord with your will.

Lord Jesus Christ,
you enter our world to vanquish sin and to
    push back the power of Satan.
Give me strength to break with every form of
    sin and evil.
Free me from all the oppression and
    sickness and darkness
that sin has brought into my life.
Let me share in your victory
and know even now the joy of
    your resurrection.

Holy Spirit of God,
pour forth your healing gifts upon your church.
We ask that wonders and signs and
    miracles and healings
be manifested among God's people.
Equip and empower us to heal the sick,
to comfort the sorrowing,
to break every form of oppression.

OTHER PEOPLE'S PRAYERS

Even as I turn to you for healing, Lord,
I also offer you all of my own
   suffering and pain.
I offer it to you, Father,
in unison with the suffering of your
   Son Jesus on the Cross.
Let my suffering be as a prayer,
not only for me but also for all those
   who need salvation in Christ,
especially my family and those close to me.

In life or in death, Lord,
in strength or in sickness,
I am yours.

John Bertolucci, an American Catholic priest with an evangelistic ministry.

16 God of compassion,
you take every family under your care
and know our physical and spiritual needs.
Transform our weakness by the strength
of your grace
and conform us in your covenant
so that we may grow in faith and love,
We ask this through our Lord Jesus
Christ, your Son,
who lives and reigns with you and
the Holy Spirit,
one God, for ever and ever.

The Liturgy of Anointing within the Eucharist.

17   We pray for all who continue your
       healing ministry
throughout the world,
and thank you
for churches and individuals,
who take seriously and joyfully
their calling to bind up the wounds
in lives which are torn by ill-health,
in communities which are divided
    by bitterness,
and in families which are shattered
    by the death of love.

*The Word and the World: Prayer Handbook of the
United Reformed Church.*

18 Lord God, I know that this is a sick world and that my sins are part of this sickness. I also know that, though I do not deserve it, Jesus, your Son, has died for my healing. Through the crucified and risen love of Jesus, I am able to come to you, Father, and to find in you forgiveness and peace, and eternal life. Stir in me the healing power of the Holy Spirit; both for my own wholeness and so that I may myself be a channel of healing in the world, in the name of Jesus.

Roy Lawrence, an Anglican priest of the Church of England.

19 Lord Jesus, born of so young and tender a mother, look down in thy mercy and compassion on all waiting mothers, that peace and hope may be with them, and that thy great love may cast out fear. Let thy light shine upon them and the strength of thy loving Spirit be in them, that the life born of them may be dedicated to thy service, for thy name's sake.

A prayer for expectant mothers, used at the former Mothers' and Babies' Hospital Woolwich.

20 Father, we pray for those who are mentally ill,
for all who are of a disturbed
    and troubled mind.
Be to them light in their darkness,
their refuge and strength in time of fear:
That they may put themselves into your hands
and be filled with your peace.
Give special skills and tender hearts to all who
    care for them,
and show them how best to assist in your
    work of healing;
through Jesus Christ our Lord.

Ministry to the Sick

OTHER PEOPLE'S PRAYERS

SOURCES OF PART 7

I wish to express my gratitude to the following for permission to reproduce material of which they are the publisher or copyright holder.

1 Lucien Deiss, *Early Sources of the Liturgy*, Geoffrey Chapman, 1967.
2 *A Manual of Eastern Orthodox Prayers*, SPCK 1945.
3 *The Gelasian Sacramentary*, ed. H.A. Wilson, Oxford University Press 1894.
4 *Hymns Ancient and Modern Revised*, William Clowes and Sons, Ltd. 1950.
5 *Uncommon Prayers*, ed. Cecil Hunt, Hodders 1963.
6 *The Book of Common Prayer with Additions and Deviations proposed in 1928*, Oxford University Press.
7 *Chronicles of Convocation*, 1935.
8 Leslie Weatherhead, *A Private House of Prayer*, Arthur James Ltd.
9 Joanna Ernst, *The Life of Dorothy Kerin*, The Dorothy Kerin Trust.
10 *The Hodder Book of Christian Prayers*, ed Tony Castle 1986.
11 Malcolm Boyd, *Are You Running With Me, Jesus?* Heinemann 1965.
12 George Appleton, *One Man's Prayers*, SPCK.
13 Jim Glennon, *Your Healing is within You*, Hodders 1978.
14 John Richards, *Twenty-Four Healing Prayers*, Renewal Servicing, 1984.

15 John Bertolucci, *Healing: God's Work Among Us*, Servant Books, USA 1987.

16 *Pastoral Care of the Sick: Rites of Anointing and Viaticum*, International Committee on English in the Liturgy, Inc. 1982.

17 *The Word and the World*, United Reformed Church, 1986.

18 Roy Lawrence, *Invitation to Healing*, Kingsway 1979.

19 Author unknown. As far as I know this prayer has never before been published.

20 *Authorised Alternative Services: Ministry to the Sick*, Central Board of Finance of the Church of England, 1983.